Don't Explain

HARPER & ROW, PUBLISHERS

NEW YORK

Cambridge
Hagerstown
Philadelphia
San Francisco

London
Mexico City
São Paulo
Sydney

1817

Don't Explain
A Song of Billie Holiday

FRANK DRIGGS COLLECTION

by Alexis De Veaux

Library of Congress Cataloging in Publication Data
De Veaux, Alexis, 1984–
    Don't explain.

    Bibliography: p.
    Discography: p.
    SUMMARY: Presents a prose poem recounting the life of the
American jazz singer affectionately known as Lady Day.
    1. Holiday, Billie, 1915–1959—Juvenile literature.
2. Singers—United States—Biography—Juvenile literature.   [1.
Holiday, Billie, 1915–1959.   2. Singers.
3. Afro-Americans—Biography)   I. Title.
ML3930.H64D5   784.5′3′00924 (B) (92)   78-19471
ISBN 0-06-021629-8
ISBN 0-06-021630-1 (lib. bdg.)

ACKNOWLEDGMENTS

So many times our art has gone
unrecorded/making it often impossible
to do research or find documentation
for what has been left behind/thank God
Billie left us her music

I am deeply indebted to all writers and
critics who ever wrote about Billie especially Hettie Jones, John Chilton and Ralph J.
Gleason for their excellent research and
literary contributions to Lady Day's image;
among those I wish to extend a special
thanks to are the Staff of the Schomburg
Center for Research in Black Culture (Harlem New York City); Lionel for his tapes; my
family; my grandmother Ruby Hill for her
prayers; Liz Gordon for remembering what I
once said years ago; Audrey Barnes for
listening to me read the last few pages; all
the folk who gave me their memories tales
and opinions and told me to make sure I do
right; Valerie Maynard and Carole Byard
who helped me through some rough mo-

ments; all my friends who understood why I had to unplug the telephone; Billie herself who sat up with me those last few nights typing and told me the ending was all wrong and go do it over/which I did; and above all Gwendolen Hardwick who got that stick-with-you love and encouragement when I'm going crazy and she doing all the cooking.

for Billie
for Gwen

Swing, Billie

This is a long song
Sing it
A song about Billie Holiday
These words are notes
High and low
Hard and hot
Soft and cold
This is the jazz
Sing it.

Billie Holiday wasn't her name when she was born
April 7 1915 in Baltimore Maryland.
It was Eleanora.
And her mother Sadie Fagan was 13 and a maid.
And Sadie wasn't married
to Eleanora's father Clarence Holiday.
Peddling papers at 15
he was taking trumpet lessons after school.
Clarence was crazy about his trumpet.
And Sadie was crazy about that boy Clarence.
But Clarence's High Society Black family did
not approve
of him fathering no scandal
especially in Baltimore in 1915.
So Eleanora got her mother's last name.
And Sadie got another job as a maid.
And Clarence got tired of his mother saying
Eleanora wasn't his baby/but what could he do.

With no money and a baby to feed Sadie Fagan
had to work double hard to make ends
meet.
She scrubbed floors.
Washed laundry.
Did the cooking.
And kept her mouth shut when other people
hollered

YOU ARE LATE TO WORK/ she was humming
don't cry baby don't you cry
hushabye baby don't cry
we gonna make it sugah pie
hushababy hushababy
don't you cry
while all the time knowing she and Clarence
wanted to be a family living in one house.

And that's just what they did.
When Eleanora was three years old Sadie
and Clarence got married and moved into
an old house on Durham Street in Baltimore.
Sure they were young and broke and he loved
his trumpet but
he was crazy about Sadie and her baby.
What else mattered?

Then the Army called for Clarence.
They sent him overseas to Paris.
He had always wanted to play trumpet serious.
While in Europe he was exposed to poison gas.
It ruined his lungs.
So he took up guitar instead.
He wanted to be a musician.
It was in his blood.
That was all he wanted really.

Music.
Music any way he could get it.
Music broke up his family.
Music and the First World War.

To Eleanora growing up with Sadie
was full of roller skates baseball climbing
trees in their backyard/cousins
being poor negro Victrolas cooing jazz
wanting white silk socks
& patent leather shoes
and hot dogs in the segregated
5&10 of Baltimore.
And the colored school.
And not liking her name Eleanora.
Her father called her Bill because
he said she was a tomboy.
She liked his name for her but she wanted it
pretty.
Like Billie Dove her favorite movie actress.
Billie Dove was beautiful to Eleanora
sneaking
in the back way
of movie houses to save her dimes.
Eleanora made her 'do like Billie Dove's.
Painted her nails.
Changed her name

from Eleanora to Billie.

When the War was over Clarence Holiday
came back
to Baltimore interested in music only.
He joined a band called McKinney's Cotton Pickers.
And went on the road touring.
He never lived with Billie and Sadie again.

When the War was over Sadie kept her job
in a factory making Army overalls and uniforms.
And for 15¢ at 8 years old Billie scrubbed
white marble steps plus bathrooms or
ran errands for 5¢ or 10¢ either one.

In the meantime she left school
in the 5th grade
to grow up a big boned–big breasted
grown up child
men mistook for a woman in those
days in the South:

one day Billie came home from school
a neighbor
was there
his name was Mr. Dick see Mr. Dick
Billie's neighbor where's

momma Billie said
at the hairdresser Mr. Dick said she told me
to wait for you she told me to take you
someplace to wait for her
come on let's go Billie
went with Mr. Dick down the street see
see Mr. Dick see Mr. Dick and Billie going
down the street
to a lady's house
the lady opened the door come in she said
your mother called on the telephone your mother
say she is going to be late it got later and
later and later and Billie fell asleep
Mr. Dick took Billie into a back room
he put her to bed
see Mr. Dick get into bed
with Billie Mr. Dick that was his name
he had a jealous girlfriend she went to Billie's
house and told
Billie's mother to keep Billie
away from her man don't be silly
Sadie said
Billie ain't nothing but a child
and the jealous woman
screamed she's with him
now right now so Billie's mother

made Mr. Dick's
girlfriend take her and a policeman
to the house
where Billie had lain down to sleep and wait
for her mother who would be late and when
the police and Sadie
and the jealous girlfriend
arrived at the first lady's house
Billie was already crying and bleeding so
the police took Billie
and Mr. Dick and Sadie
down to the police precinct
and Mr. Dick was in his 40s Billie was 10
and the police sergeant did not
believe Billie
was only 10
none of the police did when they looked
at her
well formed big breasts and big bones and
nobody believed
she was only 10
with a body like that
Billie enticed Mr. Dick they thought and
put her into a cell 2 days
passed
then they went to court in court Mr. Dick

was sentenced
to five years
Billie was sentenced to a Catholic institution
for girls until she was 21 but
Billie's grandfather and Sadie
got a lawyer
and some help from some rich White folk
Sadie was working for
and they got Billie out of there when
Billie
was 12 it was 1927

Now that Billie was home again
Sadie did her best
to give Billie a good life
with fine things.
But there was never enough money.
To get it Sadie went North to find better
work as a maid while Billie was shuffled
from relative to relative.
And the only thing that kept her happy
during that time was listening to music
by herself
and imitating popular singers.
All day all night if she could Billie
would sing girl sing.

The first time she heard Bessie Smith
and Louis Armstrong
bluesing on an old Victrola in the parlor
of a brothel
where she worked as a cleaning girl
Billie was mesmerized.
Louis doing "West End Blues" was the first time
she'd ever heard
anybody skat
through sassy feeling music.
The way Bessie did it she drawled.

It wasn't just the music either.
It was the way Bessie Smith carried herself
bigger than life.
The newspapers and grapevine said she was
living in her music
full and legendary.
Billie wanted that style and feeling for herself.
Wanted it straight from Bessie's mouth from
Bessie's throat
from down her gut those words
making those
blue sounds.

At 13 Billie was living with her cousin Ida.
Her mother was in New York working as a maid.

9

When Cousin Ida died
Sadie sent Billie a one way ticket North.
She was glad she was leaving the South.
The South leaves scars
hard-to-shake-off/colored only
no colored allowed stealing yessir no ma'am
can I wash
your floors for you lady
we don't sell niggras nothin here scars.
Was the North really the Promised Land?
Was it really like she'd heard?
With a train ticket in her pocket a small
suitcase
a basketful of fried chicken and
hard boiled eggs
Billie put the South behind her
for now
like so many other
Black people then.
Leaving the South for a better life North.
It was a dream.
A dream thousands and hundreds dreamed.
Where you going girl
We going North
Where you going man
Taking that big train North.

When the train she was riding
reached Penn Station on 34th Street
in New York Billie felt her blood boiling over.
For New York New York was Big City Times.
And Black folk making good.
Instead of getting on the train to Long Branch
New Jersey
where her mother was to meet her Billie decided
Long Branch
could wait.
There was someplace else she'd heard so
much about.
HARLEM.
THE MECCA OF MAGIC FOR BLACK FOLK
FROM EVERYWHERE.
She had to see it first.

>   *Harlem is the jazz they say*
>   *Sweet Harlem*
>   *Sidewalks are coal black marble*
>   *Silver stars glisten on pavements they say*
>   *Black gals dangle on the arms of beaus*
>   *Oh/sweet sweet Harlem in the late 20s*
>   *Rent parties and speakeasies*
>   *Florence Mills and Marcus Garvey*
>   *Black Swan Records and Bert Williams*
>   *The Harlem Renaissance*

Cut the rug   jug-a-lug
Broadway playboys in Little Africa
Nella Larsen and W.E.B. DuBois
Oh girl   oh sweet sweating Harlem
And Zora Neale Hurston
And The Elks fancy parade
Dicty Harlem of flappers and furs
Of Kid Chocolate
Strivers' Row
Of Southern folks up North
Congested tenements by the hundreds
Going back to Africa on the Black Star Line
Colored Nurses and Colored Cops changing Harlem
Changing into a Mecca
A dream thousands of hundreds dreamed.

And to Billie it was also a dream.
A rich dream.
For this was the life she wanted to be part of.
Those fancy dressed Black folk.
Two tone brownstones and sidewalk politicians.
Restaurants night clubs cabarets
and no more white marble steps
to clean/no more
White folks' kitchen floors to mop no sir
she was through with that nickel here—
a dime there
life

in Baltimore.
So when she and Sadie finally found a place
to live together
in Harlem in 1929
Billie felt this was where she belonged
with Sadie/at last.

Sadie and her daughter settled down
to life scuffling
up North in a small apartment
139th Street.
It was their first home together
since Billie was a little girl.
Being family to each other was important to them
and when Sadie wasn't working
and Billie wasn't getting the feel
of Harlem's
musicians
and dance halls
and dance bands
they stayed home nights
and Billie taught Sadie how to read
while practicing her singing.

And it wasn't too long
before their place became a combination
hotel

boarding house soup kitchen and after hours
joint where
good meals came cheap then.

Sadie had a big heart and she loved people
especially musicians
especially Clarence Holiday.
Loved him long after he had gone
and remarried to a West Indian woman
name Fannie
long after when he became a ladies' man
in Fletcher Henderson's Band
at the Roseland Ballroom
dodging Billie
who called him daddy out loud momma needs
a coupla dollars.

In 1930 the Great Depression came
with bread lines
for the jobless hundreds in Harlem.
It was the dead of winter.
While working as a maid Sadie took sick.
Their money began to run low.
The rent was overdue.
An eviction notice had been served.
Billie and her mother would be put out unless.
That night Billie hit the streets looking

for work.
At 15 she had never had a job doing anything
except cleaning.
And she was not going back to that/no sir.

Hungry and desperate she walked Seventh
Avenue
from 139th to 133rd Street
past restaurants and people warming in
bars
too busy to notice her begging in every
after hours joint
glamorous cafe or regular spot
she stopped in
I need a job mister
Can you wait tables girl?
No sir
Can you short order cook girl?
No sir
Can you?
No sir
What can you do?
SING?
Got a jukebox here girl/we don't need no singer.

168 West 133rd Street was the last place
she stopped at.

A joint called Pod's and Jerry's.
I needa job mister.
What can you do girl?
I can dance.

She couldn't.
She was awkward and embarrassed.
Scared stiff.
She needed 45 dollars/rent money before morning.
The piano player urged her to sing if she could.
Clear and sorrowful in a lazy low tempo
Billie sang
"Trav'lin All Alone."
The club's audience was stunned to ever hear
music seeping
from lips the way hers did.

When the evening was over Billie took
the rent money home
to Sadie and the good news:
She had a job *singing* for 18 dollars a week.

For 2 years Billie enjoyed singing
at Pod's and Jerry's.
It was always crowded with big tipping customers.
She was a newcomer with a brand new style.
Beautiful sassy and cool.

She had her own way and she was young enough
to be stubborn:
I am a singer jack got that?
I am not a strip tease.
I ain't picking up no tips between my thighs.
He got a tip for me?
Let him look me in my eye.
Some of the other singers
felt she was too highbrow.
Acting just like a lady they said she was.
A Lady.
Miss Lady they nicknamed her/now she was "Lady."
Too good to do what we do for tips.

Singers were a dime a baker's dozen in the early 30s.
When Billie Holiday flexed her vocal cords
she pulled strained teased and jazzed
popular music.
She was new and scared but Lord could she sing.
"Give me a song I can feel and it's never work,"
she said.

Did you say the blues?
No baby Billie don't sing no blues.
Billie sing a long Southern city girl song.

Listen jack
Listen to that lazy drawl
Hold the note back

Listen
Listen up jack
Listen to that crazy/lazy drawl
Hold it
Hold it
Hold the note back
Awwww shucks girl
Through my ears   let your music crawl

In 1933 when Pod's and Jerry's changed its name
to the Log Cabin
it became a hot spot
for show business people gathering there.
Folks like John Hammond the jazz aficionado
and Mildred Bailey
the jazz singer
and songwriters producers promoters and agents
looking for talent.
One night Joe Glaser came to hear Billie sing.
Joe Glaser was Louis Armstrong's
and Mildred Bailey's agent.
An agent could do a lot for a newcomer.
Especially a newcomer with a unique sound

like Billie's.
After he heard her sing Joe Glaser
signed Billie for a contract
on the spot.
He knew she had the jazz/knew she wasn't afraid
to sing it.

After she signed with Joe Glaser
Billie's singing career
struck high notes.
In club after club all over Harlem.
The more she sang the better she got.
The better she got the more word spread.
What's the word?
Thunderbird.
Who's the dazz?
LADY'S
The Jazz.

Harlem night life buzzed with the sound
of Billie's name
and music.
With Black folk who loved and envied her genius.
And White folk in ermines and emeralds who loved
their chauffeured rides uptown.

Billie was hot stuff now.

Her reputation was growing.
She was young and beautiful.
She could sing and she had class jack.
She knew how to style with her sequined
gowns
and slow time singing.
Onstage she was
hot beige and devastatingly satin.
She was mesmerizing and witchful.
Buxom and big boned she was a Black woman.
Wild and low throated sulphur and molasses.
Flamboyant.
Slicing words in untouchable patterns.
Hungry and in need.
Illegitimate and tender sassy.
Oh so sassy
For real.

After a while Billie began to feel
singing in clubs was hip but.
Most clubs catered only to those small audiences
who could afford
to patronize them.
Small audiences meant small recognition.
Billie wanted more than that.
She wanted her music played on radios
everywhere

in   arlors
or   ∍.
So   ıstry began to blossom
sh   cians
sa   build
a
m   ır audience.

It ∖   ɔdman who asked Billie
to   ﹍ ıırst record with him
af   nɛard her singing at the Log Cabin.
He was impressed.

At the Columbia Studio downtown on
Broadway
between 57th and 58th Streets the band was
ready and waiting.
Billie stood stiff.
She had never sung into a microphone before.
Her mouth opened.
No jazz came.
Calm down Lady one of the musicians told her
ain't nothing to it
but to do it.
Billie opened her mouth again
there was no music.
The band fidgeted.

What's the matter girl
you ain't got enough nerve to?
Say what? I got nerve I got plenty nerve.

And with that she relaxed into song.
That afternoon November 27 1933
she and Benny Goodman's band
recorded 2 tunes for Columbia Records.
One was "Your Mother's Son-in-Law"
a bluesy pop ballad
and the other was Benny Goodman's own
matter-of-fact tune
"Riffin the Scotch."
Nothing became of the record at that time.
Columbia paid Billie 35 dollars that's all.

Not long after that first recording session
Billie cut
more than half a dozen tunes
on the Brunswick label
with Teddy Wilson's band.
Billed as a vocalist she received only 30 dollars
for some
of her most popular tunes
like "I Only Have Eyes for You"
"Miss Brown to You" and "I Cover the Waterfront"
not to mention

"What a Lil Moonlight Can Do-o-o-o-o."
It was a flawless recording and Billie was proud.
But it was a year later
before the album really began to sell.
And when it did Billie fought the record company
to get more
money for her work.
She deserved far more than 30 dollars
she knew that.
30 dollars came nowhere near
the energy and feeling she had to put out
for this business was her whole life now
and it was certainly
worth more than 30 plain
damn dollars.
But Columbia Records refused to give Billie
another dime.
Until a friend of hers Bernie Hanighen
a musical director with the company
made a lot of noise in her behalf.

The record company retreated under pressure.
They offered Billie 75 dollars
for the two sides she'd recorded.
No more no less.
There was no such thing as royalties then.
The 75 dollars was a flat fee.

Payment for the songs she sang *and* the songs
she had written.

To them Billie was *only an artist* that's all.
The artists made music the music company
made money.
And that's what happened to Billie.
And to Bessie Smith.
And that's what happened to Nina Simone ask her.

Making records did not support Billie so
she continued to do her act in the clubs
uptown.
Singing at the Hotcha Club one night
she got sick.
And Bessie Smith—in town briefly—filled in.
For Billie this was unbelievable.
Her idol/who she always wanted to sing like
The Great Bessie Smith
at the Hotcha Club.
Billie quickly recovered the next night
and went onstage
eager to show Bessie
in the audience
some of her best stuff.
She even sang one of Bessie's songs:
"Gimme a Pigfoot and

a Bottle of Beer."
But Bessie Smith
was never in the habit of
congratulating
young singers.
She walked out of the Hotcha Club that night
after Billie's show
without a word.
They never saw each other again.

It was 1935.
America was between wars.
Harlem was between jobs and riots.
Billie was between 20 and stardom.
Still singing all hours
at the Hotcha Club when the manager
of the Apollo
and Lafayette theaters/Frank Schiffman
came to see who everybody was talking about.
Billie sang pretty that night.

After the show Schiffman offered Billie
an engagement
at the Apollo Theatre
that coming April for 50 dollars a week.
She was thrilled to the bone and scared.
It took guts to sing at the Apollo.

Only the best dared.
The Harlem folk
had no use for singers who couldn't swing.

All night up singing at the Hotcha Club
with no sleep
she was to open at the Apollo that morning at 10.
Pigmeat Markham/a bodacious comedian
had warmed up the audience.
It was Showtime at the Apollo and time
for the singer.
Billie lost her nerve.
She kept running to the bathroom full
of butterflies and stage fright
finding one excuse after another.
Until Pigmeat Markham pushed her out
onto the stage.
Her legs were rubber stilts
her knees wooden door knockers.
Her palms were sweating.
She held the microphone for dear life.
Opened her mouth
and sang "When the Moon Turns Green."
It was okay after that she felt better.
And when she did "The Man I Love" Billie
tore the house down.

The audience loved the way she sang her voice.
Patterns of dark embroidered textures.
Gabardine and silk.
Danced along the vocal scales with
hypnotic ease.
Low notes/were mysterious midnight sounds
moonlight and smoky Harlem joints
Or tenor and alto saxophones crying
Or the mystical African moan
of oboes and balofones.

Billie Holiday painted folktales for her
audience.
Gentle and lazy in a satin white gown.
Head tipped backward/jeweled down.
Handsome fingers lightly snapping.
Her lips puckered between the gracious
folds of stories.
Of the songs she acted in.
Funny or serious this Billie Holiday was
so dramatic
onstage
she could sauté sizzle or steam.

When Billie first started singing
professionally
in the clubs and making records

her father thought such a voice too
raw for the public.
He said Billie would never make it as a singer.
She'd starve first.
Have to beg for jobs.
Be a failure and admit it.
Clarence Holiday
had little faith in his daughter's gift.
Perhaps he was jealous.
Certainly he did not like her style.
Or the songs she acted and sang.
However when Billie was invited back
to the Apollo that same year
Clarence visited her
at the Hotcha Club to wish her luck.
It was the first time he ever came anywhere
Billie was acting out her songs.
The first time he noticed she loved to be
onstage.
To charm the audience.
Excite them to squeeze please burst in song.
Slice open their lives.
To reveal the love the pain.

Every chance she got
she let out the actress in her.
Once she played the wife and the maid

on a daytime radio
soap opera.
Switching from one voice to another
Billie learned to develop
her dramatic sound.
True Romances paid her 15 dollars a day.
Playing mob scenes in a movie on Long Island
the month before she reopened at the Apollo
Billie met Paul Robeson.
Also in the movie
Paul Robeson's extraordinary acting and singing
talents fascinated Billie thrilled with
the drama and glamour
surrounding movies and movie people.

A few months later she accepted a part
in a film featuring
Duke Ellington and his Band.
Symphony in Black in 1935 was a musical
brimming with talent.
To sing a blues number Billie played
the sweetheart of a ladies' man.
Even on film
she transformed a minor singing part
into an event.
With a sense of rhythm about words she knew
which ones to put

together.
When to pause for emphasis.
Which phrases were most powerful or
scorching.
Her voice was an instrument whose notes
she played with a poet's hand.
"She could re-shape the bleakest melody,"
someone once said.
It was true/she could.
And in the wee hours of September 25 1937
when Bessie Smith
was in a car accident on a Mississippi road
and bled to death and her blood was her music
and it had to go someplace it went to Billie
in her throat
I believe that do you.

So Much Jazz

BROWN BROTHERS

In the early days of her career Billie
recorded sang and made popular
over 200 songs
a lot of them "mainstream" tunes.
Played on the radio in barber shops & beauty
parlors cafes
& night clubs these were
the popular numbers everyone knew.
They were easily accepted/their lyrics
offended challenged
or blamed no one for war
or world tension.
"Pennies from Heaven" is one of those songs.
Billie sang it light and sarcastic.
With her voice she made fun of the silly words
of the country
and people who could produce such a song
in the face of hunger
everywhere.
She teased it with a subtle swing.
Mocked it in a friendly voice.
Took those meaningless words
and turned them around.
Changed the melody line.
Sang it *her* way/brought the song to life.
Freed it in her throat/any song was reborn.

Songs that were more serious she treated
with fragile care.
She wanted her listeners to see and feel
beauty in the painful
story she was singing.
With words closer together
or farther apart a serious texture
changed the tone to change the melody.
In one song she could be hoarse or dry or
butterfly oboe or bell.
She was always Billie Holiday the haunting
jazz legend.

During recording dates
when short one tune to record
the other musicians often told Billie to try
a blues in A flat.
Go as far as she could go with it.
Billie sometimes made up the words to a song
right there on the spot.
Other times she usually had to select her tunes
from batches of sheet music
the more well known singers refused to record.

Nevertheless/she was young and new
to the business.
Often moody.

Offstage she was shy unsure of herself.
Am I as good as people say I am?
Am I better than that?
Who else sings the way I sing?
I'm good ain't I?
Ain't I?

A kid with a 5th grade education.
On her way to becoming the greatest jazz
singer ever.
But many bandleaders did not always
understand
or dig her style.
It was too "different" for them.
Too creative.
She can't follow my music they said who
can follow hers?
Who ever heard of a *woman* singing the way she do
all fresh
and classy.

In September 1935
Billie's career was riding a steady horse
to the top.
She opened at the Famous Door club
run mostly by musicians
some of whom knew her quite well.

The White audience at the Famous Door did not
appreciate her
singing glamorous style.
They wanted entertainment—loud and bawdy.
They did not want
to take serious her subtle artistry.
Many paid her little attention.
Others openly insisted she "sing something else."

The lack of respect made her uneasy.
Between sets Billie was not permitted to mingle
with the customers
sit at a table or at the bar.
That was the club's policy.
She was just another singer
to the White-musician management.
A Black girl singer at that.
She had to sit upstairs alone in the foyer
just outside
the club's toilets
reading comic books/it was hard to sing
in that atmosphere.

Though a young singer
she was already a sensitive artist.
Impolite crowds unnerved her for she was
not yet

able to handle
uninterested audiences.
Four days after she opened at the Famous Door
her show closed.

Perhaps Billie would have been better off
working for Black
managers and agencies.
But during the 1930s
no Black agents could book Black talent
on a national basis.
The White agents and managers cornered
the market of entertainment
outlets.
So Billie Holiday and other Black musicians
(Black agents or not)
often found themselves at the mercy of White
businessmen
with the experience money
and connections
to make-or-break Black talent.

The following year Billie's manager Joe Glaser
arranged
a job for her
at the Grand Terrace Ballroom in Chicago.
It paid 75 dollars a week working

with Fletcher Henderson's Band.
The same band her father had worked with
years before
as a struggling musician.
Billie left New York in June 1936
feeling on top of the world.
Her good feelings did not last long
after they reached Chicago.
Ed Fox the manager of the Grand Terrace
did not appreciate
Billie's style.

BILLIE

ED FOX (annoyed)

You wanted to see
me Ed?

Yes. Tell me—
where'd you learn
to sing?

I didn't learn it.
I just do it.

I don't like it.

I don't sing to please
you.

I'm paying you.

What's that
supposed
to mean?

My customers don't

BILLIE

Slow?
What do they
want—
merry-go-round
music?
I know what I'm
doing.

Just like that?
I want my money
jack.
Pay me before I
leave here.

I said PAY ME MY
MONEY—

I WORKED AND I
WANT
MY MONEY ED.

ED FOX
like it.
They say you sing
too slow.

Not for my money.
You're finished.

Pack your things
and get out.

Go learn
how to sing
like normal people.

Get out of here.

She was raging mad
throwing furniture all over his office.
Ed Fox threw insults nasty insults.
Then he fired her with no salary
no nothing.
Billie went back to New York flat broke.
She went to see Joe Glaser.

JOE GLASER   BILLIE (puffing mad)
What do you
expect?
You've got to speed
up
the tempo Billie
baby—

                              WHOSE SIDE ARE
                              YOU ON JOE?
                              THEIRS OR MINE?

You've got to sing
the
hot stuff Billie.
None of that jazzy
moody business.
At least not all the
time.

                              I'm going to sing how
                              I want to sing.
                              My way—dig it?

By now most club owners uptown knew of Billie
and she could work almost anywhere
as much as she wanted to.
She continued to sing her way the artistry
of the jazz
that possessed her.

With recordings and bookings coming
steady now Billie
and her mother moved
to a new apartment over a small vacant
restaurant on 99th Street and Columbus Avenue.
Sadie had always wanted to open a real
restaurant.
Successfully she convinced Billie
to invest some money in her
dream idea.
So Billie gave her mother the money to open
and stock Mom Holiday's.
Unfortunately Sadie had no business sense.
She gave away more than she took in.
And Mom Holiday's soon became a parlor with
a kitchen for musicians
friends strangers or
any hungry body in need of a meal
or two dollars till better days.

The restaurant business proved to be
a source of irritation
between Billie and Sadie.
Tension rose
as Billie found herself sinking much of her
ready cash
into an expensive dream.
A big spender who gave away money and
never saved, she was often flat broke.
One day she needed money.
Although she and Sadie were not speaking then
she was sure Sadie
would give her a few dollars
from the register.
But Sadie refused to lend Billie any money.

She had her reasons and she wasn't budging.
No matter how much Billie screamed
and carried on.
Sadie stood her ground.
And Billie left the restaurant angry and hurt.
Whispering an old proverb "God Bless' the Child
That's Got His Own"
she walked out.

Still angry 3 weeks later she wrote and
recorded

her famous
"God Bless' the Child."
One of the many tunes she was to write
in her lifetime,
it became a standard number
in Billie's repertoire no matter
where she sang.

42

There were mixed feelings in the music business
about her genius
by the time she was 21.
Some musicians respected and loved her sound
followed her
from club to club
for a chance to jam with The Lady.
Others like Stuff Smith envied the power of her
dignified style.
At the Onyx Club on West 52nd Street
he and Lady played separate shows.
Their styles were an exciting contrast
for the audiences.
Whenever he played his violin the smell
of his hunger
to be better than her seeped out
betwen B flat and C sharp
halftones of jazz:
I hunger   You hunger   He/she/it hungers
We all hunger for a job to eat sleep rent
for self-preservation

Stuff became jealous of Billie's popularity
with the club's regulars.
After all he
had been playing the Onyx Club longer than she.
The Stuff Smith Sextet had brought good business

and the club's owner knew it when
Stuff backed him against the wall:

Billie's onstage too long
Billie's getting too many encores
Billie's milking the audience
Billie Billie Billie's got to go
It's me or Billie man
Without me there's no show.

Stuff Smith or Billie Holiday.
It was a hard decision to make.
With his business thriving the club's owner
reluctantly
dismissed Billie.
In December 1936 she was asked to come back
when Stuff Smith
and his band went on tour.
Although she did she was deeply scarred
by the distances
she felt growing between herself
and other musicians.
They don't like me
They don't like my music
They don't like my style
Why what is it
I'm as good as them ain't I

And better than some/ain't I
But they don't like me

Billie recorded the tune "That's Life I Guess"
shortly after the Onyx Club incident.
Relaxed and in total control of her voice
she was not bitter.
Pain can be washed out with a song.
Pain can become jazz digested and transformed.
She had taken the whole affair in her stride.
Billie proved she could create
triumph out of crisis out of need to.

When she finished her return engagement
at the Onyx Club
she went to work at a joint called the
Uptown House
on 134th Street and Seventh Avenue.
The Uptown House was owned by Clarke Monroe
who had a younger brother
named Jimmy who was handsome
the way Billie liked men
but there would be plenty of time
for a handsome man
like him/later.

Right now there was someone else.

Someone special.
He was born in Woodville Mississippi
August 27 1909.
He was the son of a carnival musician.
He spent most of his young life traveling
and playing
in his father's band.
He was dark skinned and shy.
He was a beautiful gifted jazzman.

In 1934 while he played with Fletcher Henderson's
band in New York
other musicians criticized his saxophone sound:
You call that music jack?
Where'd you ever learn to play?
Who taught you rhythms like that?
Where you from man where you from?
What's his name?
Lester Young.

Lester Young and Billie Holiday first met
at a recording session
in January 1937.
Each one a unique and talented musician
they worked together well.
He had a horn he sang like a voice.
She had a voice she played like a horn.

During the recording session Lester
stood behind Billie his cheeks
puffing breath winds through his sax.
Billie heard the soft tropic breath tiptoe
behind her words.
She loved to hear Lester's sound beneath her own.
That day she recorded "I Must Have That Man"
one of her best recordings ever.

From that moment Billie and Lester
became bosom friends.
Two kindred souls
in love with each other's music.
Some friends are lovers who are not who
blow pretty solos behind each other who
sit at the back tables of night clubs
to appreciate who
stand in the corners of jam sessions just to
celebrate the beauty.

It was Lester who took Billie
to the jam sessions uptown
in all night joints after the usual clubs
had closed.
Musicians improvised to the sound
of creativity in jam packed
sessions where Black jazz was played no

holds barred.
Even though White musicians came uptown
to sit in with the Black
musicians there was no need
to cater to the tastes of White managers
or White audiences.
For the Black musicians raw jazz
sparkled in the hoodoo of jazz.

Lester had been living in a hotel in Harlem.
The hotel was not to his liking.
It worried him and made him anxious.
One day he asked Sadie if he could move
in with her and Billie.
There was certainly enough room
in their railroad flat
and both Billie and Sadie liked the idea
of having a man around.
So when Lester moved in he brought
his rich music and changed
Sadie's name to "The Duchess."
In the cabaret atmosphere of their apartment
Billie had a secondhand
piano at one end and Lester had his horn
at the other and between them
The Duchess had her kitchen and
the sound of their friendship

blowing in her ears.

Often broke and hungry together
they were inseparable.
They loved the same music food ideas musicians
mother-Duchess.
They loved each other so much like sister
and brother they gave
each other new names with new images.
Between friends a name given
is a form of ritual love.
Art and blood.
A circumcision of the past.

Because he was a great man to her
Billie renamed Lester:
"Pres" was short for President.
And then Pres took the Day out of Holiday
and began to call her
LADY DAY.
LADY DAY.
Statuesque and effervescent.

Men were storms moving in
and throughout Billie's life.
She was to witness the damage of high speed
storm winds moving

uprooted trees 3 months after meeting Lester.
It was March 1 1937.
Billie was working at Clarke Monroe's Uptown House.
It was 10 minutes before showtime
in the packed darkened club.
The hall telephone rang.
Someone answered it
someone called Lady to the phone.
Someone said it's Dallas Texas.

DALLAS TEXAS	BILLIE
Hello? Is this Eleanora Billie Holiday?	
	Yeah who's this? What do you want?
Are you Clarence Holiday's daughter?	
	What is this—20 questions? What's it to you?

During World War I Clarence Holiday
was a private in the Army.
He served in France and suffered gas poisoning
while fighting.
Gas permanently damaged his lungs.

From then on Clarence Holiday always needed
careful nursing   whenever he got sick.

While touring Texas with Don Redman's Band
he caught pneumonia.
In Texas the hospitals were segregated.
Clarence Holiday went from hospital to hospital.
None of them would treat him until
he found a Veterans' Hospital.
Then he had to prove he'd served
in the United States Army.
Then he had to prove he had bad lungs.
When they admitted him (to the colored ward)
they finally treated him   too late.
The pneumonia had set in.
He haemorrhaged in a bed they gave him
and they notified
his next of kin.

BILLIE   DALLAS TEXAS
What's it to you
I said.
Who's this?

                    Dallas Texas.
                    Calling to tell you
                    your father has just
                    died.

Magnificent and huge
were the ancient trees/the Baobabs
of Africa who uprooted
and flung themselves
against the walls of her brain.
Hurricanes begot tornadoes.
Chaos begot elephant cries.
Lady felt the storm/her father passing.

Clarke Monroe happened to be standing nearby.
He took the telephone from a stunned Lady
and made all the funeral arrangements quietly.
Billie walked out onstage.
She did not want to cry or mourn.
So she sang.
She opened her mouth closed her eyes and sang
for the passage
of Clarence Holiday.

Lady regretted she had not gotten to know
her father better.
Both struggling musicians
they had never been close.
Still they had shared a personal
and musical history.
Although he had often denied her as a daughter
he had come

to let her know he loved her.
And he loved Sadie Fagan too.
And Sadie had never loved anyone
that way ever again.

Lady was still working at the Uptown House
stagnating
at a promise of 35 dollars a week getting 15
or 18 depending
while Count Basie's band was on tour first
in Kansas City
and then in Pittsburgh.
Basie's band did not excite the Pittsburgh
audiences for some reason.
John Hammond the record producer
who was financially backing the Basie Band tour
decided
what the group needed was a female vocalist.
One with a strong exciting sound.
Who could intoxicate audiences
and band members alike.
Who could help make the tour a financial success.
Lady Day he thought was the perfect choice.
He offered her 14 dollars a day.
And asked her to leave the Uptown House
for the road.

The thought of touring with a band
of young jazzmen some of whom
she knew and getting paid
ignited her romantic imagination.
With hardly a second thought
she "joined Count Basie's Band
to make a little money and see the world."
But the "world" was not as romantic as Lady was
from inside
the windows of a Blue Goose bus.
For 2 years she played cards and shot dice
to keep entertained.
She drank heavy and smoked constantly.
Passed miles of roadside diners.
Caught quick naps in hostile hotel rooms
where there was no privacy.

No money for costumes to be bought
gowns to be cleaned and pressed.
No extra money for meals or room fees.
Pay for it out of your salary Lady.
Pay for it out of my salary?
How much you think 14 dollars a day can buy?
Especially since I ain't no penny pincher.
I spends money lavish.
I always do man.
What I don't spend directly on myself

I gambles baby.
Despite the inconveniences
Lady enjoyed working with the Basie
band musicians.
Her powerful singing style
broadened the band's sound.
Though she usually sang with small combos
the shift from a small band
atmosphere to big band rhythms posed
no problems
for Lady on the road.
Town after town she sang in sleazy
riffraff joints White hotels
and colored dance halls.
Two or three shows a day on little or no sleep.
Little or no rehearsal time to belt out her tunes
with that inimitable
Lady Day stamp:
Lazy gentle fingers snapping gowned down star.
Straining her voice using poor equipment.

Yet Lady was never to escape who and
what she was.
A Black woman singing with a Black band
on the road in 1937.
She soon discovered what the Black minstrels had
discovered a century

before her:
Neither the South or the North had much use
for Black entertainers.
Who didn't sing and dance the way
White audiences felt they should
sing and dance like Sambo whoever that was.
Hip shaking eye rolling teeth chattering
Mambo Sambo.
What was all this other stuff?
This moody bluesy stuff coloreds were calling
jazz?
Hmmph.
Not down here not our town.
Not Detroit neither.

Only the best of the accepted best
played the Fox Theatre
in Detroit.
Playing the Fox Theatre meant better facilities
big money greater recognition.
It was a big time gamble
and the stakes were high.
Lady's salary went from 14 dollars a day
to 300 a week.
For a Black entertainer money
was what you won there.

Each night the show opened with a chorus line
of rhinestoned women
dancing.
Costumes of sequined feathers
pale and soft and glamorous.
Underneath extravagant lights.
A line of glamorous dancing White women's legs
in Detroit.
A line of graceful swinging Black men musicians.

The audiences began to squirm and complain:

THERE ARE WHITE WOMEN HALF NUDE ONSTAGE
WITH BLACK MEN THEY SAID
KEEP THE NEGROES IN THEIR PLACE ONSTAGE
AND OFF
WHO'S RESPONSIBLE FOR THIS SACRILEGE
AND RAPE
WHO'S RESPONSIBLE

The management of the Fox Theatre was
frightened
of a possible riot.
They insisted the show had to be changed or else.
The next time the chorus line appeared
there were no extravagant
dancing lights sequined songs or feathered steps.

In the "new" chorus line were White women
in Black masks
wearing mammy dresses.

It was an insult to Lady Day Count Basie and
the Band each night
at the Fox Theatre.
But the audience was satisfied to be entertained
at the expense of Black artists.
The show went on.

Soon after/the theater managers began to
look at Lady with a funny eye.

THE MANAGERS	LADY DAY
You're too light skinned.	
	WHAT??
Yellow.	
	Well I'll be damn—
Somebody might mistake you for white—	
	Is this DETROIT or DOO DOO town Alabama?
especially if the light—	

THE MANAGERS   LADY DAY

GET AWAY FROM ME

doesn't hit your face
just right.

What in the heck is this
you giving me?

Black greasepaint to
darken
your face.

I AIN'T USING IT SUCKA.
I AIN'T NO DAMN
MAMMY
RAG DOLL SO GET OUT
OF HERE.

You want to work or
not?
You are under
contract.
If you refuse we can
sue.
You won't work
anywhere ever.
None of you.

Under contract and legally at the mercy
of the theater managers
Billie's answer held the careers of Count Basie
and the others

in the palm of it.
In her hotel room she stood before the mirror
and smeared
the dark greasy wax over her face full of pain.
"There's no business like show business," she said,
"you have to smile
to keep from throwing up."

A Black woman in blackface.
This was the tragedy.
Not the life she lived.
Or the men she loved.
Or the women after men left.
Not that.
But the narrow attitudes of entrepreneurs
and birds of prey
who carved the jazz
feasted on the song
ate without saying Grace.

As time went on Lady began to be disappointed
by the touring experience.
She had not been prepared
for the spiritual abuse she was to suffer.
Her physical strength began to wane.
She became moody temperamental.
She refused to compromise now and

sing in joints
where owners treated her with no respect.
Why should she/already a legendary singer
she had style and class and she knew music
was a healing magic.
As a vocalist she was unparalleled
she could sing anything anywhere.
But the excitement was gone now.
Lost down a Blue Goose road.
There were constant problems between Lady
and the band's management
over Lady's songs costumes drinking
and smoking habits.
One thing became another until Lady Day
and the Count Basie Band parted
bitter company early in 1938.

When Lady began to work again
she took to the small clubs
and joints around town.
Glad to be working she secretly hungered for
something dramatic.
Situations that promised unknown excitements
ignited the actress
in her.
Conflict whether personal or professional
always found expression

through Billie's music.
Events and words became dramatic stories
became the jazz Lady Day
needed.

When the chance to tour with Artie Shaw's band
came along
Billie went on the road again.
This time with an all White band to Chicago
and Boston and South in a Rolls-Royce.

She was the only Black member of the band.
The problems she had with Count Basie
were light stuff compared
to her days with Artie Shaw.
On the road she was refused entrance
to diners and restaurants.
She ate most of her meals
from brown paper bags in the car
driving through Chicago
and Boston
hotels would not rent her a room
in Kentucky Baltimore Cleveland
and back to Detroit to sing at the Fox Theatre
light enough to sing without greasepaint
this time
she was not allowed access

to a public bathroom in most places
she was not allowed any of the comforts
due a star.

Many times the fellows in the band stuck up
for her.
They refused restaurants and hotels
that would not serve her.
Many times however they did not.
Because they were dog tired.
Had traveled 600 miles.
Played 3 gigs in 2 days.
Needed sleep needed food.
Needed not to be bothered.
Because they were White and didn't care.
Because they were White and cared.
Because the country was race tense
everywhere they played.

The late 1930s found Lady Day an artist
of stupendous powers.
A woman of disturbing beauty/a
"whole jazz scene by herself."
That was her problem businessmen said.
She was "too artistic."
More often than not song pluggers
for music publishers wanted

Artie Shaw's promise he would not
let Billie Holiday sing their songs.
Why not? Lady's the best thing that ever
happened to this band.
Because.
Why?
Because she's too damn creative.
She doesn't stick to the written melody.
We don't want an interpretation of the song.
None of that feeling stuff she does Artie.
Just somebody to sing the words
that's all understand?

Artie Shaw always took Lady Day's side.
But there was one time he didn't October 26 1938.
The Shaw band opened at the Lincoln Hotel
in New York City.
The billing read ARTIE SHAW & BILLIE HOLIDAY
in the elegant
Blue Room Ballroom.
Every night the show was broadcast on
radio coast to coast.
It was a big break for Billie.
And Sadie got a kick out of sitting home
listening to her Billie sing.
But once more Lady was not allowed
to visit the bar or dining room.

Once more she was to spend hours
in a dark room upstairs
waiting to be called for her numbers.
The Management pressed Artie: It's not just
her color it's her style
too slow too serious.
Lady found herself singing fewer songs.
Sometimes one song all night either before
or after the band
was on the air.
And when she refused to change her singing style
they took her off the air completely.
So when the hotel manager insisted she
enter the Blue Room
through the back kitchen door Lady hit the ceiling.
Either I come through the main entrance
or I ain't singing Artie.
Why not Billie what difference does it make?
I can't man
Not after what I been through on this tour
Not in New York City/not home
I've had it Artie I quit.

Slowly the Jazz Queen
had begun to learn a painful lesson:
She was a well known experimental
vocalist/an artiste

whose sound had changed the orbit of music
and she was Black
was the wrong color and the wrong sex and
she was not to be
granted the status or respect she deserved.

Of all the musicians and folk around her
only Lester Young
understood how she felt.
A genius too he knew no one
could invent melodies then
the way he did.
Light in tone
as the sprint of gazelles
the sound of surprise
an excursion into beauty.
But like Billie he was brilliant moody and shy.
And his music was far/so far ahead
of other musicians.
And he felt alone.
He drank gin and port mixed
to numb the lonely feeling.
Became addicted to alcohol.
Moved out of the apartment
he shared with Billie and The Duchess.
Though he and Billie were still close friends
they saw each other less and less.

1939.
Billie made a monumental decision.
To sing with dance bands was not her style.
By now jazz was big band big sound big
business.
Managers and White musicians
laid claim to the market.
Jazz became Swing.
Music is music they said.
All over 52nd Street Harlem's "race music"
became money flowed
into jobs that paid others.
At radio stations and recording studios they
stopped calling it
JAZZ
was whorehouse music they said.
Black musicians could play it uptown
in juice joints and all night
jam sessions but make a living?
No indeed.

Money in Harlem was tighter than before.
The Great Depression gnawed at the spirit
everywhere.
Clans and tribes of Southern Black folk
come North were hungry still.
Thousands out of work

on bread lines
on corners.
Resentful and restless
some became Communists in the fight
for civil rights.
Others joined Unemployed Councils
to walk in Hunger Marches.
Others refused to give up.
Harlem was suffering.
And Lady Day would sing for anyone
anywhere as long as
they paid her.

During this time a new night club appeared
in the bohemia
of Greenwich Village.
On the corner where West 4th merged
with Washington Place
off Sheridan Square Cafe Society opened.
With John Hammond's strong recommendation
the club's owner
Barney Josephson signed Lady Day.
At Cafe Society Billie's career soared
to new rhythms uncharted.
For 2 years there she was a success
a celebrity and underpaid.

———

A liberal integrated atmosphere the new club
seated only 220 people.
Pressed together between small tables
low lights and cigarette
smoke the rich and friends of the rich
paid to see to hear
the flamboyant Lady from Baltimore
with gardenias in her hair
stars in her lips under her tongue.
She was moonlight singing pretty.

One night at Cafe Society
a poet was in the audience.
Lewis Allan was a schoolteacher also
and a fan of the Lady's.
He had written a poem "Strange Fruit"
he wanted Lady to sing.
It was a haunting tale of the South
and lynchings of Black women
and men and the smell of burning flesh.
That night Lewis Allan gave the poem to Lady
after her show
was over.
Lady sat down with the paper in hand
and read and reread
the angry words.
They moved against her eyeballs

in disturbing pictures.
She saw the pain and suffering
of helpless families helpless
before slave owners plantation owners
rope carrying men.
When the club had emptied of customers
she and Lewis Allan
and a songwriter friend Arthur Herzog transformed
the poem into song.
"Strange Fruit" became a featured number
for Billie Holiday
while she worked at Cafe Society.

Excitement crackled through the air inside.
Each night the tiny club was packed with Black
and White hip folk
waiting.
For Lady's rendition of "Strange Fruit"
had become news throughout
jazzland.
Word traveled on the lip of drums and
the teeth of saxophones.
Have you heard it
Have you heard
Saxophones grow from gardenias behind the ear.

The house lights hushed down.

Through the intimate dark Lady Day appeared.
In a white shimmering gown and white gardenia
her beige face
bore rivers of a song known centuries
before she was to sing it.
Prominent cheeks rose like drumbones
beneath her lush satin skin.
Lady Day paused when the music stopped.
Tipped her head back.
Let the drama/Black life unfold:

She sang and she acted and she sang
the words/became scorching

gestures leaping off her tongue.
In 1939 in America Lady Day blew
oppressed life into the story
behind the song.
For the first time in her career
Lady Day sang a protest song.
She spit feeling into its radical meaning.
She rode the lyrics breathless
this untamed jockey
Fought
Cajoled
Seduced
Wrenched
And freed a defiant song in a dangerous
time.

With "Strange Fruit" in her repertoire
Billie's career changed
once again.
The legend grew from a premonition of splendor
to a magnificent
violent wind.
"LA GRANDE CHANTEUSE" she was called now
in the newspapers.
THE GREAT SONGSTRESS.

Lady Day unfolded her deepest feelings

every time she sang
that song.
It brought out her jazz regal and pained.
Broadened the quality of the work
she was to sing from then on.
It spread her gift wide open.
Made her reach deep.
Between one night stands and the blue truth.

It was a dangerous song in a dangerous climate.
Angry Blacks milled in the streets of
congested Northern cities.
Crime and disease spread.
Over Southern nights the sky burned
with shadows of Ku Klux Klan
men breathing beneath the hood of white sheets.
The Mason-Dixon line ran from Chicago
to the Carolinas.
America smiled through one face at the world
and spit through the other at Blacks.

This was the reality Lady Day was soon to witness.
Columbia Records/the record company she'd
been recording with
rejected "Strange Fruit."
Not on your life they said.
We'll be boycotted.

It's too inflammatory.
They won't buy it in the South.
It'll never sell.
Why can't you just sing soufflé songs?
Why can't you just be quiet about all this?

NO.
The song had begun a flood in her
opening dams of pain
and stench and chains and time crossing over
the Atlantic
the Mississippi
the Jordan River the Nile
the floodings of history
had begun to fertilize the memories
in Billie's seed.
She was determined
to record "Strange Fruit" that year.

And until she did she would not give up.
Perseverance.
That's what she had perseverance.
Step and keep stepping.
Over obstacles over nonbelievers over
no matter what.

Billie went to see a friend of hers.

Milt Gabler owned the Commodore Record Shop
in Manhattan.
It was a small but growing business.
It was the first American record company
devoted exclusively to jazz.

MILT GABLER	LADY DAY
What's with you and the long face huh? Why the long face?	
	I've got the lyrics for a great new tune Milt. A great tune. But the cats over at the studio won't let me record it. A great tune like this. Ain't that something? All the bread they making offa me. I've got to do this number Milt. I've got to.
Is it all that important to you Lady?	

MILT GABLER	LADY DAY
	Do elephants doo doo?
How about doing it for my label then?	
	Don't jive me man.
I'm not kidding. Do it on Commodore.	
	No strings?
No strings.	

"Strange Fruit" was first recorded
on the Commodore label
April 20 1939.
Backed by a small combo
led by trumpeter Frankie Newton the tune
was an immediate success among the
Black and
White intelligentsia.
Although it was kept out of close earshot
and its flip side
"Fine and Mellow" was pushed as the real hit
of the Harlem jukebox trade
the song's political message
rang clearly for Harlem's people.
This music had the power to spark an uprising
for freedom.

Music stays in the air.
It travels at the speed of breath
at the sound of light.
It is never not heard.
It can wait centuries if it has to.

Despite that the record sold well.
Billie received a great deal of public attention.
The notoriety and controversy
surrounding her newly released tune
thrust her name and image
onto the international music scene.
But Lady felt no closer to the acceptance
from the general public
she thought she deserved:
the love of all jazz musicians
the recognition in the public's eye the crush
of autograph seekers after successful concerts
the praise
the standing ovations thundering hands
clapping music to her name
nothing more nothing less than love.
At the close of 1939 Lady Day vowed
she would quit the music
business by the time she was 26
if she had not gained
the dramatic stature and fame she envisioned

was only 2 years away.
1940.
She was now a dramatic songstress.
A glamorous celebrated woman.
She had chosen a path and she was following it.
But Billie was sensitive and given to moods.
The increasing demands of night
club and concert
producers that she perform
no matter what annoyed her.
If the atmosphere was not right
she couldn't perform she said.
She just wouldn't show up.
Or she'd be late.
Or she'd sing a couple
of temperamental tunes and leave.
Still when things were right and going well
Lady Day was a disciplined
creative musician
who captured audiences all over the world.

By the end of 1941
America was to be involved in a world war
for the second time.
Blacks were again encouraged
to support the war effort.
In turn they demanded more jobs and better justice

from the government they were asked to protect.
Women were separated from lovers brothers
fathers in a chaotic
frightening time.
Men were separated from mothers children
sisters roots.
There was a lot of coming and going pain.
Nothing certain in war.
Nothing guaranteed.

Lady Day had begun to think of
her personal life more.
In the midst of this confusion
she was no closer to her goals.
Now 26 she turned her attention inward.
She had many lovers.
Some pursued her because she was "Billie Holiday."
And it boosted their own prestige
to be seen with her.
Others followed her about because
they found her brilliant and
attractive and they wanted to harness
what gold they were sure
she must be/this light
from the sun so bright.
Still others stayed around because she was
lonely and generous

and she gave away much more than she
received.
More money.
More time.
More love.

But she was lonely/far lonelier
than most could imagine.
It was a loneliness that went beyond a lover.
Went way back to 5th grade when she left school
to support herself.
Scrub white marble steps.
Give up roller skating and boxing.
Grow up in homes for girls
her mother working as a maid.
Songs growing in her bones
music in her blood Lord
Lord
Billie's music
Billie's blood.

She wanted a steady man/that year.
So while working at the Famous Door club
in New York she began
to date Jimmy Monroe.
They saw each other frequently.
Sadie Fagan did not take to him and demanded

Billie stop seeing him.
Her agent Joe Glaser did not like Jimmy either.
He encouraged her to cut the romance off but
Lady had a softness
for handsome men.
And Jimmy Monroe was young flashy and
handsome.
She liked him and she let him know
she liked beautiful men.

Jimmy Monroe's no good for you baby
Sadie Fagan kept insisting
Jimmy Monroe don't mean you no good.
You don't need him Billie/you don't
know anything about him.
So what Joe she said so what.

In August 1941 Lady Day and Jimmy Monroe
drove from New York City
to Elkton Maryland and eloped.
It was her first marriage.
It was his second.

Not long after they were married
Billie discovered Jimmy
had two habits he could not break.
The First:

One night Jimmy came home late.
He had been with another woman she could tell.
There was lipstick on his collar.
Lady saw it/he saw her see it.
He tried to explain he began to lie.
"Don't explain," she said, "man don't explain."
Don't explain an ugly scene
became a sad song for Billie.
The words fell out in heartbreak rhythms.
Several nights later she sang it
for her friend Arthur Herzog.
He played the tune on a piano.
They changed the words some/softened the
melody.
"Don't Explain" became one more
of Lady Day's standard songs
wherever she played.
It was a popular tune with women who
would not let her leave
the stage sometimes without singing it.

The Second:
Jimmy liked opium.
He smoked it a great deal around her.
When marriage to Jimmy began to fall apart
she began to smoke it too though it made her sick.
She needed something to ease the pain.

Opium did.
When she and Jimmy smoked together
they fought less.
That's how she wanted it/no fighting.
So she smoked.
So she got hooked.

Several months later although their relationship
did not improve
Billie and Jimmy left the East
Coast for Chicago and a booking
at the West Coast
Cafe Society in Los Angeles.
Billie felt good her first time in the
California sun
she could work steady make money and forget
what was wrong between her and Jimmy
sometimes.
Working at the West Coast Cafe Society
gave Billie a chance to
be in the thick of Hollywood glamour and gossip.
She was thrilled by the movieland aura excited
by the handsome
clothes of Hollywood celluloid queens.
Things were going well for Billie
making 175 dollars a week.
She spent every dime of it buying

beautiful clothes and good times.
When Cafe Society folded unexpectedly
Lady found herself
out of work and broke.
And then Jimmy got busted and she was alone.
In California with no money
with an opium Monkey on her back
she had not the slightest idea how to feed.

She headed back to New York.

Sadie was glad to see her daughter home.
Come stay with me again Billie like the old days.
Help out in the restaurant why not?
I'm sick Billie.
Momma I'm a married woman now.
I gotta man in jail.
I got problems I got to solve them.
She wanted her marriage to last.
She wanted it to be romance and songs
in the best Hollywood style.
Under pink sunsets holding hands.
A dozen red roses on a silver breakfast tray.
I love you written between stars.
Nothing in the world was like that.
Not in countries going to war.
Not among races fighting.

Or husbands and wives on drugs falling apart.
Nevertheless she kept her nerves together
working the New York
clubs.
Swing Street.
Uptown.
Downtown.
Joints like Kelly's Stables.
Cafe Society in the Village.
And The Monkey was still on her back chanting
opium
opium
Where could she get some stuff now?

Where *could* she get some stuff?
Jimmy had always gotten it before.
But he was in jail in California.
She was in New York.
Who had it who knew?

Joe Guy knew.
Joe Guy was a young musician from Georgia
fresh on the music scene.
But he knew what Billie wanted
and where to get it.
He knew how much to pay for it
and how much to charge Billie.

She often paid 100 dollars
for what someone else paid 25.
How could she know/she didn't care
as long as she had the money.

Opium has a funny smell.
It is not easy to hide this smell
in backstage dressing rooms
of small clubs or on the road.
It made her nauseous.
She wanted to feel good not sick.
She needed something less obvious to others.
The war brought with it new discoveries
in painkillers.
Cocaine and heroine for wounded soldiers.
Drugs helped them get back on the field to
fight.
American soldiers became addicted to white powders
flowed in their veins
flowed cross the Atlantic
into American harbors
into New York in
to Harlem.

HEROINE.
Heroine didn't smell on workers left behind.

Or women.
Young boys too young to be useful in the war.
Harlem writers after the Renaissance.
Black musicians who
could not support themselves needed something
to lean on.
No wonder in the 40s.
No wonder there was plenty heroine around town.

Joe Guy was good to Lady during the war.
He helped her keep the good times flowing
through The Chanting
Monkey in her veins.
Heroine is quiet and does not smell.
Heroine is needle tracks of pain on your arms.
This one's for all the race insults.
This one's for baby when you coming back.
This one's for just let me sing
what I want to sing.
And this one.
And that one.
And this.
And that.
And the more she sang the more
that Monkey hollered
feed me Billie feed me.

You making good money now Billie.
You making 1000 dollars a week.
Feed me the best Billie get it anywhere you can
The best costs money Billie spend it
On some more
On some more.

She made good money during the first years
of World War II.
But it meant little to her.
It was easy come easy go.
There was always more to get
from a new song or a new recording.
Club owners outdid each other to star Billie
on their stages.
They paid for her and they continued
to pay her generously.
What she didn't give away
she squandered just for the sheer pleasure.
On Sundays she'd go uptown and do jam
session after jam session
with other musicians for no money.
She loved to sing and she loved
to spend and give away the money she made
from it.

While she and Joe were working together

one night
Billie got an idea.
Why not form a band?
Why not?
Other musicians certainly had.
And she could have just as good a band
as anyone
with a good road manager and Joe on
trumpet.
Herself doing the vocals and some sidemen
why not?
A business venture would be a solid investment.
A week later and a few out of town
bookings under her belt
she bought a huge white bus and painted
BILLIE HOLIDAY
AND HER BAND on the side of it
and drove it uptown to see her mother
before taking off.

Sadie fussed over Billie
and the other musicians in the new bus.
She made curtains for the windows.
Fixed fried chicken sandwiches
and drinks for the road.
Warned them to be careful driving.
Wouldn't let them leave till they promised.

And when they finally pulled off
hours later Sadie stood
on the corner at 99th Street
in front of the restaurant
watching her daughter's dream band disappear.
A small frail beautiful woman she
smiled and waved good-bye.

The Billie Holiday Band
traveled to Washington DC
for their first appearance.
They opened to packed audiences at the grand
and beautiful Black entertainment palace
the Howard Theatre.
Billie was superb and the band's respect
for her style was impressive.
It was the first time on the road
she felt comfortable.
Singing with her own band
boosted Billie's confidence.
Even though she and Joe Guy
were not the best of business folk
the group's road manager
helped to keep things flowing smooth.
One night after the show
Billie returned to her hotel room
with Joe Guy.

Sitting on the bed talking
she felt a strange rip in the world
around her.
A black hole.
A suffocating loneliness waiting nearby.
It was Sadie.
Frail and sick her Sadie had passed away
that night.
With the memory of Lady
teaching her how to read.
For love was the music they had between them.
Love was their proof against pain
abandonment hungry days and nights
without music from 2 caring hands to hold
a reflection of their
history.

Sadie Fagan Holiday's death in 1944
left Billie with no close family
on this earth.
She felt abandoned.
Without a living past to smell touch talk to
where was the beginning.
Of her family before her mother and father
she knew her great-
grandmother and her grandfather
and they were all dead now.

There was no one left in the living present.
No bloodline to reflect her ancestry.
No anchor to hold on to
through coming and going men friends
through the war.
For The Monkey at her back was rich and fat.
It chanted loud and clear.
It was used to being fed whenever wherever
so what.
It sat upright on her shoulders proud and heavy.
It made her stoop.
Soon she would have to crawl.

With Sadie gone the war years were USO tours
khaki dressed
audiences young Black soldiers
parades war bond rallies.
Hypodermic needles full of platinum promises.
Singing "Fine and Mellow" or "Body and Soul."
Ration books.
Letters from overseas men hungry
for a woman's smell.
Letters with foreign postmarks.
Or American postmarks.
Like the one from Jimmy Davis.
He was in the Army and had written a tune
called "Lover Man."

He gave it to Lady before he was shipped
off to Europe.
He was never heard from again.
Billie loved the song and
she wanted to record it.
She took it to Milt Gabler, at Decca Records now.
She begged him to help her fight
to have it recorded her way/with strings
in the background.
Ram Ramirez the pianist later got all the credit
for writing
"Lover Man" but Lady said
it was really Jimmy Davis' song.
In 1944 "Lover Man"
summed up Lady Day's romantic hunger
for the right man.
To come sweep away her pain and self-doubt.
Be a buffer between herself
and the music business vultures.
A pretty man to spend her money on.
A lover man to hide fragile feelings behind.

"I spent the rest of the war on 52nd Street
and a few other
streets. I had the white gowns and the white shoes.
And every night
they'd bring me the white gardenias

and the white junk."
So the war years went for the Gardenia Lady
saying good-bye
to Sadie Fagan lonely soldiers old loves
quick loves until
a misunderstanding between Lester and herself
found a weak spot
in the seam of their friendship
and unraveled it.
Some say Lester didn't care for Billie's new habits.
Some say Billie felt Lester's friendship
had gotten too possessive
he telling her what to do.

In New York City 1946 she is 31 years old.
The Monkey she has been carrying on her back
has a vicious appetite.
It is never satisfied.
It begins to make her crawl.
The Chanting Monkey has eaten most
of her ¼ of a million dollars
she has made singing in the last 3 years.
Still The White Powder Monkey chants
feed me Billie feed me.

FEED IT OR GET RID OF IT BILLIE
THIS IS YOUR ONLY CHOICE

SOON THE MONKEY WILL SHOW ITSELF TO OTHERS
A FAT GHOST SUCKING ON YOUR
WONDROUS BEAUTY
SUCKING MUSIC FROM YOUR SPIRIT
THROUGH GLASSINE BAGS.

To get rid of the Monkey she needed help.
Discreet friends who could be trusted she thought.
Joe Glaser and the manager
at the Famous Door club where she was
working now would help her.
They agreed to put the word out:
Billie's having a nervous breakdown.
She's had too much worry and strain.
Billie's going in the hospital to cover
up the real truth.

The "hospital" was a private sanatorium
rich folk or folk
who could afford it stayed at to cure
whatever ailed them.
Right in Manhattan.
The hospital staff agreed
to accept Billie for a 3 week stay.
They charged her 2000 dollars.
They promised to keep everything confidential.
They agreed to cure her.

The "cure" was a tough one Billie
had not been prepared for.
The Monkey did not want to leave.
It had become accustomed to the warm
soft of her back.
Each night it clung to her screaming
bloody blue murder.
Ghost arms making circles
in the air white powder screams.
Bloody blue bloodcurdling sickness.
Give her pain.
White monkey sitting on her brain.
Got no eyes got no lips full of sucking beauty.
Monkey got no music monkey see monkey do
monkey die.

I love my man, I'm a li-ar if I say I don't.

Ab7 Db9 Ab Bbm7 Bm7

I love my man, I'm a li-ar if I say I don't.

Cm7 Bbm7 Eb7 A7 Ab6 Fm7

But I'll quit my man, I'm a li-ar if I say I won't.

When Billie left the sanatorium she thought
she was cured.
Through with drugs she looked forward
to being her own woman.
Free to start all over
she wanted nothing to do with The Monkey
when word leaked from the hospital:
Billie Holiday that sassy Black woman
has a drug problem.
They didn't say *had* they said *has*.
And Federal Narcotics Agents
sniffing for any news
of big time entertainers breaking precious laws
began to follow her.
Even though she was not
on drugs she felt they followed her
everywhere
she went to.
Every club she played at.
Every concert every cafe.
From New York to Hollywood and back.
Everywhere she went she felt
the blank gray face of a Federal man
waiting.
To wreck her last nerve keep her jumpy in doubt:
Am I clean?
I'm sure I'm clean

Check my pockets check my lipstick case
I haven't taken any stuff today
I'm sure I haven't
Have I?

Not to let real or unreal fears
get the best of her Lady
kept on working the New York club circuit
until she left
for Hollywood the following year.
With the help of her agent
she got a part in the movie *New Orleans.*
It featured Louis Armstrong and his band.
By now Louis and Lady had become good friends.
He had come to appreciate her music
and the contribution
she was making to jazz.
Louis Armstrong got to play himself in the movie.
Billie got to play a blues singing maid.

"I'd fought my whole life to keep
from being somebody's maid,"
she said, "and after making more than a million
bucks and establishing
myself as a singer who had some taste
and self respect, it was
a real drag to go to Hollywood

and end up as a make-believe maid."

Billie hated the maid's role.
When she realized the contract
had already been signed she hated it
even more.
Unfortunately she needed the money.
To walk out now might mean the end
of her chances to work
in Hollywood again.
Reluctantly she agreed to play a role
she felt degraded her image
as Billie Holiday.
The dramatic and glamorous songstress of jazz.
She wanted to be recognized
for her extraordinary sound.
Praised for her innovations and voice control.
Loved for her rhythms and pain.
But not in Hollywood in 1946.
Hollywood had its own image of the Black woman.
After all/weren't all sassy Black women
mammies mulattos and maids?

In the evenings when she left the movie set
Lady worked the club circuit.
Often up half the night singing
she'd dash over to the set for a 6:00 AM call.

It was a rough schedule and she got little sleep.
At night she was Billie Holiday.
During the day she was a maid.
Having 2 personalities disturbed her and
Billie fought believing
herself a maid the whole time she worked
on the film.

When work on the film was over
Billie stayed in Hollywood
singing at various clubs.
She was on top again as La Grande Chanteuse.
She played the leading role in every song.
Each night the famous and unfamous
came to listen to her
riffing and spicy jazz.
Billie Holiday could hit no bad notes
she could sing no bad tunes.
For Hollywood audiences Billie was a silver star.
Whether day or night the legendary streets
filled with handsome
women and beautiful men who counted her
in their star filled lives.

Despite her thrill at being in Hollywood
it was not easy to stay
away from drugs.

There was no one close who really cared
about the pressure she felt.
With contracts to honor.
Agents to support.
Musicians to pay.
An image of glamour to maintain.
Bloodsuckers to feed.

Blues

BETTMANN ARCHIVES, INC.

Blue blue
Lady who?

Though she had succeeded
in getting rid of The White Powder Monkey
lately she had noticed it again.
Every time she went to the store the bathroom
or out to eat.
Hanging on to her ankles.
Grinning through fanged teeth.
Feed me Billie feed me.
Who cares if you feed me.
It's just you and me Billie.
You and me.
All the while she continued to make records.
Club dates kept her voice in good form.
Yet a new sound began to break beneath
the notes/suffering.

It was during this time that Lady Day's music
took on a profound quality.
It came under her voice no surprise
the way winter comes under fall.
Penetrating her glamorous image.
It was the Bessie Smith in her blood coming out.
Through every struggle it was
music to reflect her life.
The blue mood of frustration of sex of sanity
got to stay sane.

Billie let it out through tunes
like "Good Morning Heartache"
"Deep Song" and "Solitude."
She was without direction without Sadie
there was no one she loved.
Singing moved her closer to freedom
one day coming.
It put a shape and a handle on her pain.
Gave her suffering a form she could deal with.
Lonely mornings before concerts
in strange cities.
At night under cover in hotel beds.
One eye open one eye closed
on the road from this town to that.
Cigarette after cigarette.
She hated being alone.

And The Chanting White Monkey knew this.
Turn to me for company it said Billie turn to me.
Turn to me.
And she did.
Once more have mercy she did.

In May 1947 Lady Day and Joe Guy
and several other musicians
were working at the Earle Theatre
in Philadelphia.

Louis Armstrong and his band
were working there also.
When the show closed a week later
everyone felt good.
It had been a good show
and it had closed on a good note.
Afterward when the musicians left the
empty theater
on their way to the hotel
Billie felt something was not right.
Perhaps it was just her nerves.
Perhaps it was the blank faces of gray men
she thought were always
following.
Maybe it was The Monkey's chanting shadow
over her shoulder who knows
what it was she felt tickling
at the back of her neck who knows
what it was.

By the time she finished dressing
she was convinced it would not
be a good idea to go back to the hotel.
Oh come on Billie the others ignored her.
You and your hunches.
Get a drink.
What's wrong with you Billie you outta your mind?

What do you mean don't go to the hotel.
What about our clothes money everything?
Leave it.
Get the car.
Drive back to New York.
Something ain't right Joe.
But the others insisted Billie was just jumpy.
When she met them later at the hotel
it was brimming with police.
They were looking for Billie.
The fear of being arrested drove her to panic.
Escape, The Monkey chanted, escape.
Don't let them catch us Billie.
We must escape.

She had never driven a car before that night.
She took the wheel.
And the black rented limousine
carrying a frightened Lady Day
a confused chauffeur and Lady's dog Mister
pulled up in New York City
several hours later.

She had escaped.
For the time being she was safe.
The next night she opened a show
at the Onyx Club on 52nd Street.

She was scared and Monkey sick.
She knew The Law would come for her soon.
The Law did come.
The Law sat patiently in the audience at the
Onyx Club.
The Law did not want to interfere
with her making money for the Club's owner.
The Law waited a whole week.
The Law did nothing but grate on her nerves.

When her engagement at the Onyx Club
was up that week
The Law busted her.
For buying and using drugs
in Philadelphia and
for carrying concealed drugs from New York.
They took her back to Philadelphia.
It did not matter to them that Lady was sick.
And tired of The Monkey chanting in her ear.
No ifs ands or buts Lady never sold any drugs
not once in her life.
So what/this is a Federal crime The Law said
a Federal crime is
any unusual act
executed without the express written permission
of the Federal government paragraph by
paragraph.

That May 1947 *The United States of America
versus Billie Holiday*
in Philadelphia was a short quick trial:

1. Billie was sick and alone.
2. She signed away her right to have a lawyer.
3. The judge was not sympathetic.
4. The District Attorney's office
   had gathered evidence against The Monkey.
5. Because certain Monkeys are illegal
   she pleaded guilty.
6. And was sentenced to one year and one day
   in the Federal Women's Reformatory
   at Alderson West Virginia.

She had been put away to be cured
of her addiction.
She was expected to repent and be rehabilitated.
She scrubbed the floors of kitchens.
Worked on a farm picking tomatoes
and other vegetables.
She shoveled coal.
Slept in a segregated cottage.
Ate in a segregated dining room.
Never sang one living note in jail.

Not one song.

Not once the whole 10 months she was there.
(2 months off for good behavior)
"I couldn't have sung if I wanted to.
The whole basis of my singing is feeling.
Unless I feel something, I can't sing.
In the whole time I was there
I didn't feel a thing," she said later.

Bags of fan mail sent every day
she was not allowed to receive.
Precious gifts came from all over the world.
Thousands of telegrams and copies
of her albums sent to cheer her
up were all sent back unappreciated.
She was in jail.
With no room for glamorous gowns.
Sonorous songs.
High paid jobs at the best clubs in the country.
For 10 long isolated months Billie pretended
there was no life blood
flowing in her music.

Ten days after she was released from jail
Lady Day was booked
into Carnegie Hall in New York City
for a Saturday midnight concert.
It was a frightening idea.

A concert at Carnegie Hall?
Suppose people had forgotten her.
Suppose she ended up singing to an empty hall.
Suppose suppose suppose she couldn't sing.

In Carnegie Hall every available space was sold
to fans and believers.
Still Billie was nervous.
Why are so many people coming to hear me sing?
They just want to see what a jailbird sings like
I'm sure.
She had not used her voice in a long time.
There were songs she sang so easily before
she was now afraid to sing.
The notes/the notes.
What about those high notes?

Saturday night before Easter 1948.
Thousands of fans are turned away from inside.
3 thousand more fill the plush Carnegie Hall seats.
Squeezed onto the famous stage
are 400 people sweating in anticipation.
Lady Day the legendary Queen of Jazz
has come back to sing for them.
Come back with her electrifying style
to transfix and transform
the listening ears.

The moment came.
30 pounds heavier she appeared on stage.
In a rich black dress a cluster of white
gardenias floating above one ear.
Elegant and simple.
LADY DAY LADY DAY.

The audience was moved to its feet
thousands of hands clapping
and calling her name.
LADY DAY LADY LADY DAY
In the thunder Billie stood silent
to witness this thunder-praise.
Sweet and powerful.
To match her lightning voice
full of seances and scriptures.
Full of jazz way before the Dead Sea Scrolls.

SING BILLIE
SING THE JAIL OUT BILLIE
SING THE MONTHS MINUTES AND THE DAYS
SING BILLIE DON'T EVER LET THEM FORGET
YOU CAN SING

She sang some 30 tunes including
"Strange Fruit" that night.
When it was all over Billie

realized the concert had been
a great success.
She had not been forgotten.
People still loved her haunting hungry music.
Their presence told her:
She could be on top of the world again.
Everything could be all right.

But it wasn't.
Not so far as The Law was concerned.
Billie Holiday had committed a Federal crime.
She had been a prisoner in a Federal institution.
She had been addicted to drugs.
She had a police record.
And when Billie applied for a cabaret card to sing
in the big night clubs and small
bars of New York City
she was turned down.
No one with a police record could hold
a liquor license in New York they said.
No one can sing in a joint
where liquor is sold without a police permit.
You can sing in the theaters
on radio or television they said.
Have all the concerts in all the concert halls
you want they said.
But you cannot work in the clubs

more than 4 days without a card.
No one will hire you.

It was an everlasting blow to her career.
Although the Carnegie Hall concert
had gone well Billie
was first and foremost a night club singer.
She had built her reputation
as a dramatic songstress in them.
She thrived on the intimate atmosphere
always present.
She loved the creative freedom and spontaneity
that had accompanied
her shows in Harlem and on Swing Street.
New York City was home but she couldn't
even work the clubs here.

Working the clubs regular meant
steady money with prestige.
Time to get herself reestablished.
Keep her voice clear and flowing.
Relax.
Forget Alderson West Virginia.
Forget breaking up with Jimmy Monroe
and Lester Young.
Forget Sadie's gone.
Forget The Chanting Monkey.

Now all her plans were shattered.
Billie became terribly depressed.
She drank heavy and smoked profusely.
Cussed out old friends and made enemies
of new ones.
An angry bitter woman
she roamed the old clubs and streets
of New York.
She wanted more than anything
to sing and work and be legit.
To regain stature as an artist/in her own eye.
Be LADY.
Be Legend.

Some close friends and associates tried to
help out.
They organized a musical revue
built around Billie singing.
At the Mansfield Theatre West 47th Street
on April 17 1948
Holiday on Broadway opened.
Slam Stewart
Bobby Tucker and company
Cosy Cole drumming
black lights
Wyatt and Taylor piano duetting
a whole book of tunes

2 fancy costume changes
a sellout audience
and five curtain calls the opening night
helped to make the show a stunning success.

3 weeks later *Holiday on Broadway* closed
a wondrous success but.
Again Billie found herself out of work.
Near desperate and shut off
from the legitimate club scene
in New York, she went on the road.
Chicago.
Philadelphia.
Boston.
San Francisco.
Washington.
Clubs in other cities welcomed her
no strings attached.
Outside New York she was still the LADY DAY.
Inside New York she was a half employed
risk.

It was lonely.
Between shows out of town Billie
lived in a hotel in New York City.
After a while she got tired of the coming
and going.

She wanted to sing in New York not just sleep here.
And club owners she knew before wouldn't hire
her not even 4 days
without a cabaret card.
Desperate she tried every legal way she knew
to get work.
Until she met John Levy.
He managed the Ebony Club on 52nd Street.
John Levy told Billie not to worry
she could work at his club.
Cabaret card or not.
The police won't bother you in my club.
Sure it's illegal but don't worry Billie.
I can handle the police your ex-husband your
money everything.
Just sing Billie baby just sing.

Billie Holiday's show packed the Ebony Club
every night.
Fans and curiosity seekers came in crowds
to see her half believing
the worst.
Billie waited for the gray blank face
lurking in the audience.
There were no police to arrest her
at the Ebony Club.
And John Levy saw to it Billie Holiday

became Lady Day again.
The Jazz Queen with mink coats
to show off around town
jeweled down
Cadillacs with telephones
expensive gowns made specially for her
gloves and shoes to match
presents for The Chanting Monkey waiting
all glamour and glitter.

It was a costly mistake.
Billie soon found out.
All the money she made singing in his club
he never gave her any
in cash.
John Levy bought her everything he felt
she needed.
Clothes food an apartment drinks even friends.
He never told her exactly how much she made.
She never asked him for an accounting
she was too afraid.
She wanted to work whatever the cost.

He made sure she did nothing but
work hard at the club.
Show after show
hardly time for eating and sleeping.

Money maker
Money maker
Make that money for me honey
That's who you are now
Make that money honey maker
That's who you are
Working for me now.

Then he said work harder for 3500 dollars
at the Strand Theatre
on Broadway.
8 weeks sharing the bill
with Count Basie and his band.
5 shows a day.
7 days a week she did what John Levy told her to.
Play this gig.
Wear that dress.
Stay away from that man.
Sing this song.
No I don't want you just sign this contract
months in advance.

It was a nightmare on a merry-go-round.
Everywhere she turned the music screamed
in ugly rhythms
through her head.
Money maker

Money maker
Make that honey for me
Money maker
Money maker
Make that money for me

Tired and broke months later
she decided she could work
for John Levy no more.
After a long court battle
and expenses she could not afford
Billie Holiday and John Levy separated in 1949.

The Last Song

PHOTOFILES

Jazz had become Swing had become
Bebop in the 50s.
There was Charlie "Bird" Parker.
Ella Fitzgerald doing "Mack the Knife"
Sarah Vaughan
Oscar Peterson
Dizzy Gillespie's "Round About Midnight."
Nat "King" Cole on TV
THE FIVE SPOT
Lester Young's "These Foolish Things."
BIRDLAND
Hip cats and cool kitties and
Louis McKay.

They had met at the Hotcha Club
years before when Billie
was a teenager singing there.
She had not seen him since.
Now he was back in her life.
Handsome.
Protective.
Formal.
And courting her.
A business wise companion Louis McKay
became Billie's steady man.
Her man.
Could make her a complete person

society said then.
A woman is not a complete person
no matter who or what she has
unless she has a man
whether he loves her or not.

Billie found Louis irresistible.
To her he was romance and gingerbread houses.
A love dream to lean on.
Her Louis McKay her Lover Man.

Sometime between 1950 and 1951
Billie divorced her first husband
Jimmy and took up with Louis common law.
They were inseparable.
Louis went to all her concerts.
Chauffeured her around town.
Always hovering close by.
He escorted her to the jazz parties
and invitation only affairs.
He became what she wanted him to be.
But he could not become a mighty war-god.
He could not slay The Needle Chanting Monkey.
It came and went as it pleased.
It grew fatter.
Drank vodka and gin.
Smoked more cigarettes.

It was mighty.
It tried to swallow Billie's ancient voice.

Give it to me Billie it chanted
Give it to me
Not just yet.
She had a man and she felt happy.
She was not giving her trance-voice to The Monkey.
Not her textures of jazz pain.
Not her ballads of rage.
Not her orchestra of sacred wailings
beboping neath your skin.

But The Chanting Monkey was persistent.
It wanted Billie to submit.
It began to show itself to Billie's public.
It was ugly greedy and selfish.
Chanting Monkey appeared on her shoulders
day or night
at concerts parties walking the streets.
Old friends and running buddies who
once played with her
began to ignore Lady Day.
They turned their heads from The Monkey
stink with the smell of Lady's worst fears
The Monkey's arms wrapped around her neck
squeezed her throat until soon Billie's voice

was the Monkey's
fuzzy grainy liquid drawl.

Billie Holiday was never allowed
to have a cabaret card
in New York City.
Nevertheless she did numerous concerts
and guest appearances
at the Apollo in Harlem and Carnegie Hall.
Loyal audiences helped to make her feel confident:
Don't let the police get you down.
New York is your home.
You can make it here once again.
You can Billie.
Just keep telling yourself you can.

It was the year jazz took on a spectacular image.
Jazz festivals and extravaganzas
were created for the public.
All star concerts booked indoors and outdoors
became the way of jazz.
Audiences usually numbered thousands
on any one occasion.
Great musician after great musician
would take the stage
to entertain and perform.
And jazz the only American born music

became good listening music
became theater.
Jazz theater.
On bebop stages.
Big band spirituals from work songs
from slavery
from branches in rain forests of Africa.

In July 1953 the first Newport Jazz Festival was held
in Newport Rhode Island.
Loyal fans came by the tribes and
truckloadsful to witness
some of the best known jazz artists
in the world that weekend.
Among them were Ella Fitzgerald
Oscar Peterson
Dizzy Gillespie
Erroll Garner
Billie Holiday and Teddy Wilson.
They had come to hear to blow in the fresh air
they knew their jazz
would dance weightless.
Dizzy's trumpet teased Erroll Garner's piano.
Gerry Mulligan's saxophone cried to Ella's voice.
All day and all night all weekend.
Nothing but sweet music sweet freedom.

Then it was Billie's turn Sunday night.
Onstage to back her were Buck Clayton on
trumpet
drummer Jo Jones
Milt Hinton the bassist
Teddy Wilson on piano and Gerry Mulligan
on baritone saxophone.
Old friends wondered
Will she show up
Will she sing they asked each other
What kind of shape will Billie be in?

With a knack for doing the unexpected
just when folks expected
her to fall apart Billie sang
her most haunting that summer night.
Words of tunes she had made famous soared
and dipped late into
the evening.
Billie was the best she had been in years.
Everyone listening knew it.
Especially Lester Young.

He had been sitting in the audience without
a word.
He walked onstage.
Stood behind Billie.

Fingers poised over his saxophone.
Head bent cobalt blue in the sun.
Cheeks puffed.
Singing pretty Lester Young played.
And blew his love through Billie's song.
Jazz healed their broken friendship.
It stitched back together their high laughing
late nights in Harlem
going home.
It stitched back their A flats.
Chicken and cornbread sandwiches.
C sharps.
B blues.
Before the night was over
the Pres and Lady Day were friends
for life again.

Then in October 1953 Billie Holiday's
"Comeback Story" was broadcast
on television.
A musical biography it was a coast to coast show.
Billie was displeased with the suggestion
her career had ever
gone down the drain to come back.
Many of her friends and associates
were invited to attend.
Some came.

Some did not come.
They did not want to be publicly associated
anymore with a well known
drug user so they said the show's producers
are not paying enough money.

Tired and Monkey sick
Billie appeared on the program.
She was glad for the national recognition
she felt she more than
deserved.
Millions of people watched her talk frankly
about her life
in the South
growing up a woman
jazz
light Black skin
no momma no poppa jail
The Chanting Monkey
White laws.

The success of the television show
helped Billie to seek
other possibilities for work.
She did more radio programs
during this time she made many more
recordings.

Went on the road as much as possible.
She hounded anyone and everyone
she knew who could get her
decent work.
And in early 1954 Leonard Feather
the jazz writer offered to star
Billie in a show he had organized to tour Europe.

It was the chance of a lifetime.

Billie had known many other Black artists who had gone
overseas to work.
Those who came back testified:
The Europeans like jazz.
They are more tolerant.
They like musicians no matter what your color.
They are more sophisticated than Americans.
Go to Europe they said.
Go and be recognized.

January 11 1954 Leonard Feather's show
The Jazz Club of America
opened in Stockholm.
Besides Billie it featured folks like Red Norvo's Trio
Carl Drinkard accompanying Billie
Beryl Booker's Trio
and Buddy De Franco's Quintet.

Billie was looking good singing fine
a smashing success.
The Scandinavian audiences loved
her classic renditions
of "Strange Fruit" "Porgy" "Don't Explain"
and "My Man."
They loved her mesmerizing style
and riveting interpretations
her drama
her voice was the bloodline of jazz.

It was the same all over Europe.
Germany.
Switzerland.
Holland.
Paris France.
3 weeks on the road one country after another.
Everywhere she went/no matter what language
people spoke.
Lady Day the gutsy Lady Day dazzled them.
And they loved her full of sass and pain.
And she loved them back.
Especially in London England that February.

The *Jazz Club of America* instrumentalists
were not allowed to play
in England because it was against the English

musicians' union rules.
Billie had no problems entertaining
the English audiences and
carrying the show alone.
Calm and dignified she sparkled
with that impenetrable hip charm.
Gowned down in her lazy finger popping
fuzzy drawl
to the music of "Billie's Blues" "My Man"
"Them There Eyes"
and "Some Other Spring" she delighted crowds
in Manchester
Nottingham and 6000 people
at London's Royal Albert Hall.
There/she was the greatest jazz singer ever.
Not a jailbird.
Or drug addict.
Or freak.

Europe had been the best thing for Billie.
European audiences reassured her
that her music was still important
and still loved.
She was swamped with offers
to work in Paris England and Africa.
She could get work anywhere.
There was no need to worry.

With her spirits lifted
and her voice still powerful Billie
returned home.
Home to fans who loved her even more now.
A changing atmosphere in music.
President Eisenhower.
Offers of more money playing better gigs.
Rock and Roll.
Recognition.
American soldiers across the water in Korea.
Home to Black kids tired of segregated schools.
Tired of segregated public restrooms.
And water fountains.
And restaurants.
And trains and buses.
And you name it
we tired.

Despite her increased popularity
the lack of a cabaret card
forced Billie to accept more and more work
before huge crowds.
A nervous sensitive artist
she was always uneasy facing audiences
like the one in Newport.
She had stage fright and feared
the audience would not like her.

In night clubs and small joints
she felt better singing.
Closer to the audience she could connect
her life with theirs.
That was her style.
Up close where lies are not told.
Eyelids blink together in one rhythm one song.
My face reflects yours reflects the universe here.

But throughout this time
Billie was in need of money.
For The Monkey.
And the expensive image of a Queen
to keep up with.
Her schedule became hectic.
She accepted gigs she wasn't crazy about.
Later in 1954 she began work on an autobiography.
Jotting down thoughts on the road.
Boston.
California.
2 gigs in 1 night.
A concert date and then a night club act
right afterward.
Doing 10 or 15 songs including
"Willow Weep for Me" "Nice Work
If You Can Get It" and "God Bless' the
Child."

No time to catch her breath.
Or 40 winks.
Or 1 good meal.

Working concerts and night clubs back to back
began to unnerve Billie.
The audiences were too different.
One was impersonal/the other intimate.
Billie sang the same songs
to both audiences.
The guttural cadence of tunes like
"Billie's Blues" worked best
in the womb of a night club.
Music critics reviewing her performances
began to question her
judgment.
They said her repertoire had grown stale
the selections too
predictable.
They said Billie's defiance was gone.

Now openly afraid she began to doubt herself
more than ever.
She drank to hide it/she fed The Ridiculous
Chanting Monkey.
Fought stormy battles with Louis.
Got little or no sleep.

Month after month of wear and tear.
The glamorous peach face became puffed
with abuse.
The lips swelled.
The shoulders struggled to be proud.
In the daytime she wore long evening
gloves up the arm
to hide her Monkey scars.
She was tense and nervous.
Her voice still had that cosmic Lady Day
magic filled with
troubles and neglect.

Lord Lord Billie
Was it worth the money and the misery?

The many years of painful living erupted in a
volcano.
What wasn't clear before was clear now.
Billie Holiday was sick.
She went from plump to dreadful thin.
During her performances now she often
needed help getting on
and off stage.
Old fans began to compare a younger Billie
to the older one.
They said her voice lacked vitality.

Where are the stories from your hands?
Bring back the drama they said.
Sing some new tunes Billie.
Don't nod don't give up.
They said how much longer will it be Billie.
How much longer will it be.

So it was no surprise to anyone when
in February 1956
she was arrested again
on a drug charge in South Philadelphia.
Another jail sentence.
Another clinic "cure."
Billie swore this time
she would give up The Monkey.
And she did but it was hard.
She had tried so many times before.
The Monkey's greed had always overcome her.
Determined to win Billie dared The Monkey
once more.
A clean break meant the world to Billie.
Louis McKay meant the rest.
And to prove it after all those years
she married him finally.

Back on the performance circuit
with a fresh start during the summer

of 1956 Billie was again the center
of public attention.
With the help of free-lance writer William Dufty
her autobiography was finished and published.
A melodramatic half true half confusing account
of her life
Lady Sings the Blues helped to keep interest
in Billie's music alive.

However Billie did not like the book's title.
To her it presented a false image.
She frowned at being referred to as a blues singer.
For she had devoted her whole life to jazz.
Jazz/sweet raw elusive it was
the art and essence of her slow time rhythms.
From Baltimore Maryland to New York
all the way halfway round
the world.
Billie suffered for jazz the way
no other singer could.
And that was "Bitter Crop" she said.
That was what *her* book should be called
not *Lady Sings the Blues.*
Nevertheless she wanted her story told.
An example to anybody coming after her
who'd listen.
It was her last song.

Over the next 2 years
she mixed gin and vodka to fill
The Monkey's absence.
With no regard for her weakened health
Billie went on the road
again.
It was a rigorous schedule.
Chicago.
Singing at the House of Jazz in Cleveland.
Las Vegas with 15 tunes in her basic repertoire.
Hollywood California and Jazz City.
Always closing her sets with "Strange Fruit"
she never returned
to the stage after singing it.
On to Honolulu Hawaii.
Miami Florida.
Back to Hollywood.
Billie's voice was failing.
The warm throaty sound became dry brittle.
Central Park in the summer of 1957.
She tried to hide the singing pain.
Because she and Louis had separated.
Because she needed ready money.
Because she was tired and weak.

1958 brought to Billie an opportunity
to tour Europe again.

Billie had always wanted to go back.
She thought now of living and working
there permanently.
Why not?
In Europe she was an *artiste*
not a down and out pop singer.
Well received on her first trip she expected
nothing less
this time.

3 weeks after signing the contract
Billie was singing in Europe.
At the Smeraldo Theatre in Milan Italy.
She appeared in concert with an assortment
of comedians acrobats
impressionists and pop singers.
In that setting Billie's slow tempoed
strained performance
was not appreciated.
She was booed and hissed off the stage.
Her engagement was to last a week.
It lasted one disastrous night.

Heartbroken but not beaten
Billie refused to believe
she had lost her touch with an audience.
Shortly after she accepted an invitation

to sing at La Scala
Milan's famous opera house.
There/in one of the small halls
during a concert organized
by an Italian film producer in love with her music
Billie Holiday proved to herself
she could still mesmerize
an appreciative audience.

But the Parisian audience
at the Olympia Theatre in France
wanted Billie to work for their appreciation.
Arouse us they said.
Sing and be glamorous.
Be legendary.
Haunt us with your painful songs.
Live up to our expectations.
And when she was too weak and could not
they walked out disappointed.
Critics wrote unfavorable reviews.
Soon Billie could not work anywhere decent
in France or Britain.
She was no longer a star.
Unable to support herself in Europe
Billie returned to America.

New York 1959.

There was no Louis around.
No Sadie or Clarence or Lester Young.
For Lester was sensitive original poetic.
He longed for a beautiful world full of love
and beautiful things
but when he realized the world was not
as he wanted it
Lester made it beautiful and precious in his music
everything was C sharp and pungent B flat
tenor beauty.
At jam sessions uptown in basements
night clubs and after hours
joints hotel rooms and ballrooms and theaters
all over the world
Pres blew his sad eyed beautiful song.
But for all his original crescendoes
and iridescent notes
for all his flights into passionate melody
among solos beyond jazz journeys
beyond the ear
the dip shout hoarse glide/of his raucous
tenor laughter
Lester Young/he who had recorded over 40 songs
with the Lady
Lester
in his porkpie hat
with his tenor sax swung to the side

mouthpiece kissing his lips
drank to keep from living
in the world as it was
died at 50
in his room at the Alvin Hotel on Broadway
across from Birdland on 52nd Street
a bottle of gin and his beautiful tenor sax nearby.

Lester Louis Sadie and Clarence.
They were all gone now.
She was lonely and seriously ill.
Once the life of any party
she seldom ventured out now.
At 26 West 87th Street she lived alone
near Central Park.
A handful of friends came to visit.
Others avoided the agony of Billie's solitude.
More than ever she wanted love.
Man love sister mother love/anybody's please.

She was broke.
The thousands of thousands of dollars
she'd made singing
almost 30 years were gone.
Gone to The White Chanting Monkey.
Gone to vodka gin or brandy.
Countless handouts.

Gone to fine clothes for handsome men
given freely.
Dinners for hungry musicians/anyone in need.
Lawyers and court fees.
Clinics and costumes.
Thousands of dollars gone.

A glamorous Billie Holiday began to fade away.
Her health continued to deteriorate.
She drank a river of hard booze.
Once a high paid high class star
she now worked for whatever
she could get.
At cheap low class joints in Massachusetts.
Half filled theaters with no microphones.
Somebody's club dance.
Jobs paying nowhere near her usual concert fee.
A Masonic Lodge affair
as a favor to another musician.
The Phoenix Theatre in Greenwich Village.
She needed money bad now so she agreed
to perform.

It was May and hot.
To see what was left of Lady Day
curiosity seekers packed the theater.
Backstage Billie was weak frail unsteady.

Sick from booze she waited in her dressing room.
No one came to wish her luck.
There was no white gardenia excitement.
Not a soothing word to calm her until.

SHOWTIME
SHOWTIME LADIES AND GENTLEMEN.
Billie pulled herself together and went
onstage.
Leaning against the piano's edge
to hold herself up she sang
only 2 songs then collapsed.
In the arms of friends she insisted
she was all right.

At home friends begged her.
Please Billie
Take care of yourself
You're sick Billie you need help
Go to a hospital
My God
How long you been like this Lady
How long you been skin and bones?

Several days later Billie collapsed into a coma.
On May 31 she was taken to Metropolitan Hospital
in Manhattan.

One more time she rallied to flush
the gin and vodka river swelling
in her body.

Suffering and surely beyond recovery
she laughed and kept her sense
of humor.
Until The Law crawled under her door.
Under her bed.
Between her clothes.
Beneath her sheets.
The unmerciful Law of the United States.
The blank gray face of crawling laws
and restrictions and jails
and convictions.
That same shameless Law
that could not find Southern lynchers in the night
could not find decent jobs for the many up north
found Billie strapped to a hospital bed
and arrested her.
For possession of narcotics The Law said.
For drugs in her coat pocket
who knows how they got there
way across the room.
So the outrageous Law searched and mugged
and fingerprinted Billie
while she was strapped to the metal respiratory

equipment
she depended on to live.
Too sick to resist or get out of bed
she watched them take away
her books flowers records watched them
stand guard outside
her door waiting for who knows.

She talked of club dates.
A new autobiography.
Made jokes with visitors and friends.
She kept smiling no matter what.
Deep down/she was still Lady Day.
She'd lived a defiant life 44 years.
Fought to sing her way the music she loved.
Jazz.
Her life blood.
Jazz was her lover.
It haunted the many songs she wrote.
Inspired her incredible beauty.
Protected her mysterious gift.
Jazz gave Billie the power of flight.
On July 17 1959
her heart began to fail.
Then her liver.
Then her kidneys.
Too weak to fight pain anymore

Lady Day's spirit
went the way of legends.

BIBLIOGRAPHY

Albertson, Chris. *Bessie*. New York, Stein and Day, 1972.

Blesh, Rudi. *Eight Lives in Jazz: Combo, U.S.A.* New York, Hayden Book Company, Inc., 1972.

Bogle, Donald. *Toms, Coons, Mulattoes, Mammies & Bucks: An Interpretive History of Blacks in American Films*. New York, Bantam Books, Inc., 1974.

Chilton, John. *Billie's Blues: The Story of Billie Holiday, 1933-1959*. New York, Stein and Day, 1975.

Collier, James Lincoln. *The Great Jazz Artists*. New York, Four Winds Press, 1977.

Drimmer, Melvin. *Black History: A Reappraisal*. New York, Doubleday, 1969.

Feather, Leonard. *From Satchmo to Miles*. New York, Stein and Day, 1974.

Feather, Leonard. *The New Edition of the Encyclopedia of Jazz*. New York, Bonanza Books, 1960.

Gleason, Ralph J. *Celebrating The Duke & Louis, Bessie, Billie, Bird, Carmen, Miles, Dizzy, & Other Heroes*. New York, Dell Publishing Company, Inc., 1976.

Grant, Joanne, ed. *Black Protest: History, Documents, and Analyses from 1619 to the Present*. New York, Fawcett World Library, 1975.

Harris, Middleton A., Morris Levitt, Roger Furman, and Ernest Smith. *The Black Book*. New York, Random House, 1973.

Hentoff, Nat. *The Jazz Life*. New York, Dial Press, 1961.

Holiday, Billie, with William Dufty. *Lady Sings the Blues.* New York, Doubleday, 1956.

Hughes, Langston and Milton Meltzer. *Black Magic: A Pictorial History of the Negro in American Entertainment.* Englewood, New Jersey, Prentice-Hall, Inc., 1967.

Jones, Hettie. *Big Star Fallin' Mama: Five Women In Black Music.* New York, Viking Press, 1974.

Jones, LeRoi (Amiri Baraka). *Black Music.* New York, William Morrow and Company, 1967.

Jones, LeRoi (Amiri Baraka). *Blues People: Negro Music in White America.* New York, William Morrow and Company, 1963.

Moore, Carman. *Somebody's Angel Child: The Story of Bessie Smith.* New York, Dell Publishing Company, Inc., 1975.

Schiffman, Jack. *Uptown: The Story of Harlem's Apollo Theatre.* New York, Cowles Book Company, Inc., 1971.

Schoener, Allon. *Harlem on My Mind.* New York, Random House, 1969.

DISCOGRAPHY:

A partial listing of recordings by Billie Holiday, many
of which are available in record stores and public
libraries.

Lady Day	Columbia CL 637
Lady in Satin	Columbia CS 8048
Billie Holiday and Teddy Wilson	Columbia CL6040
Strange Fruit	Atlantic SD 1614
The Essential Billie Holiday	Verve V6 8410
Billie's Blues	Harmony KH32080
God Bless the Child	Columbia G 30782
Lady	Verve VSP-5
Billie Holiday—The Original Recordings	Columbia C32060
The Unforgettable Lady Day	Verve MGV-8338 (two records)
Gallant Lady	Monmouth Evergreen MES 7046
Billie Holiday	MGM GAS 122
Billie Holiday Sings the Blues	Pickwick SPC-3335
Billie Holiday—A Rare Live Recording	Recording Industries RIC
Billie Holiday	M2001
The Billie Holiday Story	ESP 3002
Billie Holiday—The Golden Years	Decca DXSB 7161 (two records)
Volume 1.	Columbia C3L 21
Volume 2.	Columbia C3L 40
Billie Holiday—Immortal Sessions	Sonet SLP 1000